MW01231136

2024 CATHOLIC SUNDAY MISSAL

Readings, Insight, and Reflection

Kristi k. Miller

Copyright© Kristi k. Miller

All Rights Reserved.

No part of this publication may be reproduced, stored in a retrieval system, or transmitted in any form or by any means, electronic, mechanical, photocopying, recording, or otherwise, without the prior written permission of the copyright holder.

THANK YOU

Dear Valued Reader,

From the bottom of our hearts, thank you for choosing the **2024 CATHOLIC SUNDAY MISSAL** as your companion on your faith journey. Your purchase holds a special significance, for it means you've entrusted us with deepening your connection to God throughout the year.

We poured our hearts into crafting a missal that transcends mere words on a page. We envisioned it as a bridge, guiding you towards a more profound understanding and participation in the Sunday Mass.

Knowing that this book finds a place on your nightstand or graces your family table during prayer fills us with immense gratitude. It's a privilege to be a part of your spiritual growth.

May the **2024 CATHOLIC SUNDAY MISSAL** continue to be a source of inspiration, peace, and unwavering faith throughout the year for you and your family.

With heartfelt gratitude,

The **2024 CATHOLIC SUNDAY MISSAL** is more than just a book; it's an invitation to a year-long exploration of faith. Led by **Kristi k. Miller**'s vision and the combined efforts of her dedicated team, this missal aspires to be your trusted companion on the path towards a deeper connection with God.

TABLE OF CONTENT

Introduction

Welcome to **2024 CATHOLIC SUNDAY MISSAL** a companion resource meant to enhance your personal and community Eucharistic celebrations throughout the year. This book provides a detailed introduction to the Scripture readings proclaimed at Sunday Mass, enabling you to connect with the Word of God in a more profound and meaningful manner.

As we begin on this spiritual journey together, may the words on these pages inspire and encourage you, bringing you closer to the divine presence in our lives.

Foreword

The Christian faith is profoundly based in God's Word, a dynamic tapestry woven from the stories, lessons, and prophecies contained inside the pages of Scripture. The church unites every Sunday to celebrate the Eucharist, a hallowed meal that commemorates Jesus Christ's sacrifice. During this important act of worship, the congregation pays close attention to the readings, which proclaim God's Word.

This book acts as a link between the written word and your own experiences. As you go through the pages, you will come across the selected readings for each Sunday, given in a straightforward and understandable way. However, this resource offers more than just the text; it also gives a deeper understanding of the reading's context, themes, and meaning.

Through Reflection, Insight, and Practical Applications you are encouraged to start on a path of personal discovery and faith growth. Allow Scripture's eternal wisdom to light your path, develop your connection with God, and lead you in carrying out the gospel message in your daily life.

Before we begin this spiritual journey, let us first comprehend the book's aim and structure.

About this book

"Catholic Sunday Mass Readings for 2024" is more than simply a collection of Scripture verses; it is a spiritual guide. "Catholic Sunday Mass Readings for 2024" is intended to be a useful and accessible resource for both people and religious groups.

Each week, we will delve into the assigned readings for the Sunday Mass, providing insights, thoughts, and practical applications to help you connect more deeply with God's Word. Whether you are a lifetime Catholic or new to the church, this book will guide you on your path to discovering Christ through the liturgy.

This book has the following features:

- **Complete Sunday Mass Readings:** Easily access the First Reading, Responsorial Psalm, Second Reading, and Gospel for each week.

- **Weekly Reflections:** Gain valuable context and insights into the readings with clear and engaging reflection notes.

- **Enhanced Understanding:** Deepen your grasp of God's word with insightful breakdowns that make the message even more impactful.

- **Putting Faith into Action:** Practical applications are provided to help you seamlessly integrate the lessons learned into your daily life.

- **Personalize Your Journey:** Ample space for notes allows you to jot down key takeaways, prayers, and reflections for future reference.

- **Dive Deeper**: Explore a treasury of additional resources, including explanations of liturgical vocabulary and inspirational prayers for personal study and meditation.

Whether you are a seasoned parishioner or someone who wants to learn more about the Mass, this book will help you broaden your awareness and enhance your involvement in the Sunday ritual.

Understanding the Liturgical Year

The liturgical year is a systematic celebration cycle observed by the Catholic Church. This cycle is made up of six separate seasons, each with its own accent and focus:

Advent is a time of preparation and expectation for the celebration of Christ's birth.

- **The Christmas season commemorates the birth of Jesus Christ and God's rescuing love for the world.**

- **During ordinary time, which lasts most of the year, the emphasis is on Jesus' continuous mission and teaching.**

- **Lent is a season of prayer, fasting, and repentance that ends with Easter celebrations.**

- **The Easter Triduum refers to the three most hallowed days in the Christian calendar: Holy Thursday, Good Friday, and Easter Sunday.**

- **The Easter season is a joyous celebration of Jesus Christ's resurrection and the promise of new life.**

Understanding the structure of the liturgical year allows you to acquire a better appreciation for the themes and readings presented throughout the year. This book guides you through the liturgical year, allowing you to experience the unfolding narrative of God's love and grace as revealed in Scripture.

Importance of Sunday Mass Readings

Sunday mass readings are very important in the Catholic faith. They are a cornerstone of the celebration, linking the congregation to God's Word and offering advice for everyday life.

Here are some of the primary advantages of participating in the Sunday mass readings.

- ⋄ **Develop your grasp of the Catholic religion.** The scriptures include divine revelation, including insights into God's nature, purpose for mankind, and lessons on how to live a Christ-centered life.

- ⋄ **Connect with the Church's traditions:** The readings take you through centuries of Christian interpretation and knowledge of the Bible.

- ⋄ **Encourage personal contemplation and prayer:** Reading the scriptures may help you discover purpose in your life, connect with God via prayer, and get inspiration for personal development.

- ⋄ **Create a feeling of community** by listening to and meditating on the same readings. This fosters unity and a common purpose within the religious community.

By actively participating in the Sunday Mass readings, you gain a greater grasp of the Christian faith, a richer experience of the liturgy, and a stronger relationship with God and your fellow parishioners.

How to Use This Book:

This book is intended to be a companion on your religious journey throughout the year. Here are some methods to utilize it effectively:

- ◇ **Prepare for Mass before attending Sunday Mass.**

- ◇ **Before attending Sunday Mass, consider the forthcoming readings and thoughts in this book. This will help you approach the liturgy with eagerness and attention.**

- ◇ **During Mass, follow the readings as they are announced. Pay attentive and let the words reverberate inside you. If the opening notes give any further background or information, go to the book.**

- ◇ **After Mass, take some time for personal thought and write them down. Reread the readings, reflect on their significance in your life, and examine how the message might be applied to your everyday activities. Use the book's Practical Applications and related resources to improve your knowledge and participation.**

- ◇ **Remember the readings' themes and messages throughout the week. Refer back to the book whenever you need to refresh your memory or deepen your contemplation.**

This book is also suitable for group study or faith-sharing events. Discussing the readings with others may provide useful insights and views, establishing a sense of shared learning and community.

Remember that the purpose is not only to read the words but to let them change your heart and mind. As you interact with the readings, allow yourself to be transformed by God's Word and experience the delight of living a life guided by its eternal wisdom.

Sundays in January 2024:

Reflections and Insights

Sunday, January 7th

Baptism of the Lord - Feast (US)/Epiphany of the Lord - Solemnity

Bible Readings:

- **First Reading**: Isaiah 42:1-4, 6-7

- **Psalm:** Psalm 29:1-2, 3-4, 9-10, 11-12

- **Second Reading:** Acts 10:34-43

- **Gospel:** Mark 1:7-11

Reflection:

This Sunday, observed in the United States as the Feast of the Baptism of the Lord, coincides with the Solemnity of the Epiphany in many other parts of the world. Both celebrations center on the revelation of Jesus: the Baptism marking the beginning of his public ministry and the Epiphany signifying the manifestation of Christ to the world, symbolized by the visit of the Magi.

Insights:

- Jesus' baptism signifies his solidarity with humanity and his submission to God's will.

- The presence of the Holy Spirit at his baptism affirms Jesus' identity as the Son of God.

- The Magi's journey represents the universal call to seek Christ and find enlightenment in his teachings.

Practical Applications:

- Reflect on your own baptism and its significance in your faith journey.

- Renew your commitment to living a life that reflects the teachings of Jesus.

Be open to witnessing Christ in the world around you, just as the Magi followed the star to find him.

NOTES:_____

_____

_____

_____

_____

_____

_____

_____

_____

_____

_____

_____

_____

_____

_____

Sunday, January 14th:

Second Sunday in Ordinary Time

Bible Readings:

- **First Reading:** Isaiah 49:3, 5-6

- **Psalm:** Psalm 72:1-2, 4-7, 10-13

- **Second Reading:** 1 Corinthians 1:1-3

- **Gospel:** Mark 1:14-20

Reflection:

This Sunday's Gospel recounts the calling of the first disciples: Simon and Andrew, James and John. Their immediate response to Jesus' invitation highlights the power of his call and the transformation it brings to their lives.

Insights:

- Following Jesus requires a willingness to leave behind our old ways and embrace a new life.

- Jesus calls each of us to be his disciples, inviting us to participate in his mission of love and service.

Practical Applications:

- Examine your own life and identify areas where you may be resistant to following Jesus' call.

- Consider ways to deepen your relationship with Christ through prayer, reflection, and participation in the life of the Church.

- Be open to sharing your faith journey with others and inviting them to encounter Jesus as well.

NOTES:_____

_____

_____

_____

_____

_____

_____

_____

_____

_____

_____

_____

_____

_____

_____

_____

_____

_____

Sunday, January 21st:

Third Sunday in Ordinary Time

Bible Readings:

- **First Reading**: Nehemiah 8:2-6, 8-10

- **Psalm:** Psalm 19:8-15

- **Second Reading:** 1 Corinthians 12:12-30

- **Gospel:** Luke 1:1-4; 4:14-19

Reflection:

This Sunday's readings emphasize the themes of listening to God's word and putting it into practice. The Gospel passage highlights Jesus' inaugural sermon in Nazareth, where he proclaims his mission to preach good news to the poor, proclaim release to the captives, and recover the sight of the blind (Luke 4:18).

Insights:

- Hearing God's word is essential for spiritual growth and transformation.

- Putting God's word into practice through our actions is the true measure of our faith.

- Just as Jesus proclaimed good news to the marginalized, we are called to use our gifts and talents to serve others in need.

Practical Applications:

- Reflect on your own commitment to listening to and acting on God's word.

- Consider ways to use your unique gifts and talents to make a positive impact in your community.

- Be mindful of those who are marginalized or in need and look for opportunities to show them God's love through your actions.

NOTES:_____

_____

_____

_____

_____

_____

_____

_____

_____

_____

_____

_____

_____

_____

_____

Sunday, January 28th:

Fourth Sunday in Ordinary Time

Bible Readings:

- First Reading: Deuteronomy 26:16-19

- Psalm: Psalm 119:1-2, 4-5, 7-8

- Second Reading: Hebrews 3:1-6

- Gospel: Mark 1:21-28

Reflection:

This Sunday's Gospel recounts the healing of a possessed man in the synagogue. Jesus' authority and power over evil spirits are evident as he commands the unclean spirit to leave the man.

Insights:

- Jesus has the power to heal us.

- Jesus challenges the forces of evil and darkness, offering hope and liberation to those in need.

Practical Applications:

- Reflect on your own experiences of struggling with negativity, doubt, or temptation.

- Seek inspiration from Jesus' authority over evil and remind yourself of God's power to overcome challenges.

- Pray for those facing spiritual or physical difficulties and offer them support and encouragement.

NOTES:_____

_____

_____

_____

_____

_____

_____

_____

_____

_____

_____

_____

_____

_____

_____

_____

Sundays in February 2024:

Reflections and Insights

Sunday, February 4th:

Fifth Sunday in Ordinary Time

Bible Readings:

- **First Reading:** Isaiah 58:6-11

- **Psalm:** Psalm 112:1-6, 7-8, 9

- **Second Reading:** 1 Corinthians 2:1-5

- **Gospel:** Mark 1:29-39

Reflection:

This Sunday's readings emphasize the importance of showing mercy and compassion to others, particularly those in need. The prophet Isaiah calls for acts of justice and generosity, while the Gospel recounts Jesus' healing ministry, extending compassion to the sick and marginalized.

Insights:

- True faith is not just about believing in God but also about living out his teachings through love and service.

- Showing mercy and compassion to others is a central aspect of Christian life.

- By offering our time, talents, and resources to help those in need, we can create a more just and compassionate world.

Practical Applications:

- Reflect on your own acts of charity and generosity in recent times.

- Consider ways to practice mercy and compassion in your daily interactions with others.

- Volunteer your time or resources to organizations that serve the poor, the sick, or the marginalized.

NOTES:_____

_____

_____

_____

_____

_____

_____

_____

_____

_____

_____

_____

_____

_____

_____

_____

_____

Sunday, February 11th:

Sixth Sunday in Ordinary Time

Bible Readings:

- **First Reading:** Sirach 15:15-20

- **Psalm:** Psalm 37:23-28, 39-40

- **Second Reading:** 1 Corinthians 2:6-10

- **Gospel:** Mark 8:1-10

Reflection:

This Sunday's Gospel recounts the **Miracle of the Loaves and Fishes**, where Jesus miraculously feeds a large crowd with a few loaves of bread and fish. This act highlights Jesus' compassion and his ability to provide for our needs, even in times of scarcity.

Insights:

- God is always present and able to meet our needs, even when we feel limited or lacking.

- Sharing what we have, even if it seems small, can have a significant impact on others.

- We are called to trust in God's providence and generosity.

Practical Applications:

- Reflect on the resources and talents you possess. How can you use them to share and help others?

- Practice gratitude for God's blessings, both big and small.

- Share your resources generously with those in need, even if it means sacrificing your own comfort or convenience.

NOTES:_____

_____

_____

_____

_____

_____

_____

_____

_____

_____

_____

_____

_____

_____

_____

_____

_____

_____

Sunday, February 18th:

First Sunday of Lent

Bible Readings:

- **First Reading:** Genesis 2:7-9; 3:1-7

- **Psalm:** Psalm 32:1-2, 5-7, 8-9, 10-11

- **Second Reading:** Romans 5:12-19

- **Gospel:** Mark 1:12-15

Reflection:

This Sunday marks the beginning of **Lent**, a season of preparation for Easter. The readings focus on the themes of **temptation** and **sin**, as illustrated by the story of Adam and Eve in the Garden of Eden. The Gospel recounts Jesus' temptation in the wilderness by the devil, highlighting his victory over temptation and his call to follow him on the path of discipleship.

Insights:

- We are all susceptible to temptation, but by relying on God's grace and strength, we can overcome it.

- Lent is a time for reflection, repentance, and renewal, offering an opportunity to examine our lives and recommit ourselves to following Christ.

Practical Applications:

- Reflect on areas in your life where you may experience temptation.

- Choose a specific action you can take during Lent to deepen your spiritual life, such as prayer, fasting, or almsgiving.

- Seek support and guidance from your spiritual community as you navigate your Lenten journey.

NOTES:_____

_____

_____

_____

_____

_____

_____

_____

_____

_____

_____

_____

_____

_____

_____

_____

_____

Sunday, February 25th:

Second Sunday of Lent

Bible Readings:

- **First Reading:** Genesis 12:1-4a

- **Psalm:** Psalm 33:1-2, 4-5, 16-19

- **Second Reading:** 2 Timothy 1:8-12

- **Gospel:** Mark 8:34-9:1

Reflection:

This Sunday's Gospel reading presents a challenging yet significant call from Jesus: the call to discipleship. He emphasizes the necessity of **self-denial** and **carrying one's cross**, highlighting the commitment and sacrifices required to follow him.

This can seem daunting at first, as it implies a willingness to step outside one's comfort zone, embrace challenges, and potentially face difficulties or even opposition in pursuit of living according to Christ's teachings.

However, the call to discipleship is not simply about hardship; it holds a deeper meaning and promise. By denying ourselves and carrying our cross, we embark on a transformative journey of growth and deeper connection with Christ.

This journey involves letting go of attachments that hinder our spiritual growth and embracing a life guided by God's will.

The **Transfiguration of Jesus** on the mountaintop, occurring shortly after the call to discipleship, offers a glimpse of Jesus' divinity and serves as a source of hope and encouragement. Witnessing the divine glory of Jesus reminds us of the ultimate goal of our journey: to participate in the transformation and share in the victory over suffering and death that Christ ultimately embodies.

Insights:

- Following Jesus requires sacrifice and a willingness to place his teachings above our own desires.

- The Transfiguration reveals Jesus' divinity and offers assurance of his ultimate victory over suffering and death.

Practical Applications:

- Examine your own commitment to following Jesus. Are there areas in your life where you need to make changes to live according to his teachings?

- Reflect on the challenges and sacrifices you are willing to endure in your faith journey.

- Find inspiration from the Transfiguration and draw strength from the reminder of God's presence and ultimate victory in our lives.

NOTES:_____

_____

_____

_____

_____

_____

Sundays in March 2024:

Reflections and Insights

Sunday, March 3rd:

Third Sunday of Lent

Bible Readings:

- **First Reading:** Exodus 17:3-7

- **Psalm:** Psalm 95:1-2, 6-9

- **Second Reading:** Romans 5:1-2, 5-8

- **Gospel:** John 4:5-42

Reflection:

This Sunday's Gospel recounts the encounter between Jesus and the **Samaritan woman** at the well. Jesus challenges the social and religious barriers of his time by engaging in conversation with this woman, highlighting his message of love and acceptance for all.

Insights:

- God's love extends beyond boundaries and transcends social or religious divisions.

- Jesus welcomes everyone, regardless of their background or past, and invites them to encounter his love and grace.

Practical Applications:

- Examine any prejudices or biases you may hold towards others.

- Seek opportunities to reach out to those who are different from you and show them kindness and compassion.

- Reflect on how you can embody Jesus' message of love and acceptance in your daily interactions with others.

NOTES:_____

_____

_____

_____

_____

_____

_____

_____

_____

_____

_____

_____

_____

_____

_____

_____

_____

_____

_____

_____

Sunday, March 10th:

Fourth Sunday of Lent

Bible Readings:

- **First Reading:** 2 Chronicles 36:14-16, 19-23

- **Psalm:** Psalm 137:1-6

- **Second Reading:** Ephesians 2:4-10

- **Gospel:** John 3:14-21

Reflection:

This Sunday's readings focus on the theme of **God's faithfulness and love**, even in the midst of suffering and exile. The Gospel passage highlights Jesus' declaration that "God so loved the world that he gave his only Son" (John 3:16), emphasizing God's initiative in offering salvation through his Son, Jesus Christ.

Insights:

- God's love is constant and enduring, even when we experience difficulties or feel lost.

- Jesus is the embodiment of God's love, sent to offer us salvation and reconciliation with God.

Practical Applications:

- Reflect on times in your life when you have experienced God's faithfulness, even in challenging circumstances.

- Share your faith and God's love with others, offering hope and encouragement to those who may be struggling.

- Deepen your relationship with Jesus through prayer, reflection, and participation in the sacraments.

NOTES:_____

_____

_____

_____

_____

_____

_____

_____

_____

_____

_____

_____

_____

_____

_____

_____

_____

_____

Sunday, March 17th:

Fifth Sunday of Lent

Bible Readings:

- **First Reading:** Isaiah 43:16-21

- **Psalm:** Psalm 126:1-2, 2-3, 4-5, 6

- **Second Reading:** Philippians 3:8-14

- **Gospel:** John 8:1-11

Reflection:

This Sunday's Gospel recounts the story of the **woman caught in adultery**. Jesus' response to the woman's accusers, "Neither do I condemn you; go, and sin no more" (John 8:11), embodies his message of **forgiveness, mercy, and a second chance**.

Insights:

- God offers forgiveness and a new beginning to those who repent and seek his mercy.

- We are called to extend forgiveness and compassion to others, just as Jesus did.

Practical Applications:

- Reflect on the times you have forgiven others or received forgiveness yourself.

- Be willing to forgive those who have wronged you, seeking reconciliation and healing.

- Show compassion and understanding towards those who have made mistakes, offering them a chance to start over.

NOTES:_____

_____

_____

_____

_____

_____

_____

_____

_____

_____

_____

_____

_____

_____

_____

_____

_____

_____

_____

_____

_____

Sunday, March 24th:

Passion (Palm) Sunday

Bible Readings:

- **First Reading:** Isaiah 50:4-7

- **Psalm:** Psalm 22:7-12, 18-20

- **Second Reading:** Philippians 2:6-11

- **Gospel:** Mark 14:1-15:47 (or Mark 15:1-39)

Reflection:

Passion Sunday commemorates Jesus' triumphant entry into Jerusalem and the events leading up to his crucifixion. The readings and narratives highlight the themes of **suffering, sacrifice, and ultimately, love**.

Insights:

- Jesus' journey to the cross demonstrates the depth of his love for humanity and his willingness to sacrifice himself for our salvation.

- His suffering and death are not the end, but rather the prelude to his resurrection, offering hope for new life and victory over death.

Practical Applications:

- Reflect on the significance of Jesus' sacrifice and how it impacts your life.

- Participate in your community's Passion Sunday traditions or services as a way to commemorate this significant event.

- Engage in prayer, reflection, and meditation on the events of Holy Week, allowing yourself to contemplate the depths of Jesus' love and sacrifice.

NOTES:_____

_____

_____

_____

_____

_____

_____

_____

_____

_____

_____

_____

_____

_____

_____

_____

_____

_____

_____

_____

Sunday, March 31st:

Easter Sunday - Solemnity

Bible Readings:

- **First Reading:** Exodus 14:15-16, 21-22

- **Psalm:** Psalm 118:1-2, 14-15, 16-17, 18-19

- **Second Reading:** Romans 6:3-9

- **Gospel:** John 20:1-9

Reflection:

Easter Sunday celebrates the **resurrection of Jesus Christ** from the dead. This central event in Christianity signifies victory over death and the promise of eternal life for those who believe in Jesus. The Gospel reading recounts the discovery of the empty tomb and the announcement of Jesus' resurrection to Mary Magdalene.

Insights:

- Jesus' resurrection offers hope and assurance of life after death.

- Through his resurrection, Jesus conquered sin and death, opening the way for humanity's reconciliation with God.

Practical Applications:

- Celebrate the joy and hope of Easter through prayer, worship, and community gatherings.

- Reflect on the impact of Jesus' resurrection on your own faith and life.

- Share the message of Easter hope and love with others, witnessing to the transformative power of Christ's death and resurrection.

NOTES:_____

_____

_____

_____

_____

_____

_____

_____

_____

_____

_____

_____

_____

_____

_____

_____

_____

_____

_____

_____

_____

Sundays in April 2024:

Reflections and Insights

Sunday, April 7:

Second Sunday of Easter

Bible Readings:

- **First Reading:** Acts 5:12-16

- **Psalm:** Psalm 118:14-21

- **Second Reading:** Revelation 1:1-5

- **Gospel:** John 20:19-31

Reflection:

This Sunday, also known as **Divine Mercy Sunday**, celebrates God's boundless mercy and love. The Gospel recounts Jesus' appearance to the disciples after the resurrection, offering them forgiveness and the gift of the Holy Spirit.

Insights:

- God's mercy is available to all who seek it, regardless of their past mistakes or shortcomings.

- Jesus entrusted his disciples with the mission to continue his work of spreading the Gospel message and offering forgiveness to others.

Practical Applications:

- Reflect on the ways you have experienced God's mercy in your life.

- Extend forgiveness and compassion to others, just as God has forgiven you.

- Share the message of God's mercy with others, offering hope and encouragement to those who may feel lost or burdened.

NOTES:_____

_____

_____

_____

_____

_____

_____

_____

_____

_____

_____

_____

_____

_____

_____

_____

_____

_____

_____

_____

_____

_____

Sunday, April 14:

Third Sunday of Easter

Bible Readings:

- **First Reading:** Acts 9:1-20

- **Psalm:** Psalm 116:1-4, 10-17

- **Second Reading:** Revelation 5:11-14

- **Gospel:** John 21:1-14

Reflection:

This Sunday's readings highlight the **conversion of Saint Paul**, whose life transformed from persecuting Christians to becoming one of the most influential figures in spreading the Gospel. The Gospel recounts Jesus' appearance to the disciples at the Sea of Galilee, emphasizing the importanceof love and service in following him.

Insights:

- God can work in unexpected ways to transform lives and bring people closer to him.

- Following Jesus requires not only belief but also living a life of love, service, and commitment to his teachings.

Practical Applications:

- Reflect on your own faith journey and how you can deepen your relationship with Christ.

- Be open to God's transforming power in your life and allow him to guide you on your path.

- Offer your time, talents, and resources to serve others in your community, following the example of Jesus' call to love and serve.

NOTES:_____

_____

_____

_____

_____

_____

_____

_____

_____

_____

_____

_____

_____

_____

_____

_____

_____

Sunday, April 21:

Fourth Sunday of Easter

Bible Readings:

- **First Reading:** Acts 13:14-43

- **Psalm:** Psalm 98:1-4, 5-6, 7-9

- **Second Reading:** Revelation 7:9-17

- **Gospel:** John 10:27-30

Reflection:

This Sunday's Gospel recounts Jesus' **"I am the Good Shepherd"** discourse, emphasizing his love and care for his sheep (followers). He promises to protect and guide those who follow him, offering them eternal life.

Insights:

- Jesus is the source of our security and guidance, offering us protection and direction in times of uncertainty.

- Following Jesus requires trust and surrender, allowing him to lead and care for us as the Good Shepherd.

Practical Applications:

- Reflect on your relationship with Jesus as your shepherd.

- Trust in his guidance and allow him to lead you in your life journey.

- Seek to live a life that reflects the love and care of the Good Shepherd, offering others support and guidance whenever possible.

NOTES:_____

_____

_____

_____

_____

_____

_____

_____

_____

_____

_____

_____

_____

_____

_____

_____

_____

_____

_____

_____

_____

Sunday, April 28:

Fifth Sunday of Easter

Bible Readings:

- **First Reading:** Acts 16:9-15a

- **Psalm:** Psalm 100:1-5

- **Second Reading:** Revelation 21:1-5a

- **Gospel:** John 13:31-35

Reflection:

This Sunday marks the **Sixth Sunday of Easter** in some liturgical calendars. The readings focus on themes of **mission** and **spreading the Gospel**. The Gospel recounts Jesus' commandment to his disciples to **"love one another"** as the core message and distinguishing mark of his followers.

Insights:

- Love is the essence of the Christian faith, and it is through love that we are called to live and share the Gospel message with the world.

- Following Jesus involves not only believing in him but also actively imitating his love and compassion in our daily interactions with others.

Practical Applications:

- Reflect on how you can show love and compassion to others in your daily life.

- Look for opportunities to share the message of love and hope of the Gospel through your actions and words.

- Build stronger connections with your community and

- Build stronger connections with your community and engage in service as a way to express your love and commitment to others.

NOTES:_____

_____

_____

_____

_____

_____

_____

_____

_____

_____

_____

_____

_____

_____

_____

Sundays in May 2024:

Reflections and Insights

Bible Readings:

- **First Reading:** Acts 10:25-48

- **Psalm:** Psalm 98:1-4, 5-6, 7-9

- **Second Reading:** 1 John 4:7-10

- **Gospel:** John 15:1-8

Reflection:

This Sunday focuses on the **importance of love and unity** within the Christian community. The readings highlight the inclusion of Gentiles (non-Jews) into the early Church, signifying the universality of God's love and grace. The Gospel recounts Jesus' "I am the true vine" discourse, emphasizing the importance of remaining connected to him, the source of life and fruitfulness.

Insights:

- God's love extends to all people, regardless of their background or beliefs.

- The Christian community thrives on love, unity, and remaining connected to Jesus through prayer, service, and fellowship.

Practical Applications:

- Reflect on your own role in fostering love and unity within your community.

- Reach out to those who may feel excluded or marginalized, welcoming them into your community with open arms.

- Deepen your connection with Christ through prayer, reflection, and participation in the sacraments.

NOTES:_____

_____

_____

_____

_____

_____

_____

_____

_____

_____

_____

_____

_____

_____

_____

_____

_____

_____

Sunday, May 12th (Optional Observance)

Ascension of the Lord - Solemnity

Observed only in the archdioceses and dioceses of the US states of Alaska, California, Hawaii, Idaho, Montana, Nevada, Oregon, Utah, and Washington.

Bible Readings:

- **First Reading:** Acts 1:1-11

- **Psalm:** Psalm 47:2-7, 8-9

- **Second Reading:** Hebrews 1:1-4, 9-14

- **Gospel:** Mark 16:15-20

Reflection:

This **Solemnity** celebrates Jesus' **ascension to heaven**, marking the completion of his earthly ministry and his return to the Father. The readings reinforce the hope for our own future, as Jesus promises to send the Holy Spirit to guide and empower his followers.

Insights:

- Jesus' ascension signifies the completion of his work on earth and the beginning of a new era for the Church.

- The Holy Spirit's presence ensures the ongoing guidance and inspiration of God within the Christian community.

Practical Applications:

- Reflect on the significance of Jesus' ascension for your faith and hope.

- Pray for the continued guidance and inspiration of the Holy Spirit in your life and in the Church.

- Share the message of hope and love found in Christ with others.

NOTES:_____

_____

_____

_____

_____

_____

_____

_____

_____

_____

_____

_____

_____

_____

_____

_____

_____

Sunday, May 19th:

Pentecost - Solemnity

Bible Readings:

- **First Reading:** Acts 2:1-11

- **Psalm:** Psalm 104:1-33

- **Second Reading:** 1 Corinthians 12:12-13

- **Gospel:** John 20:19-23

Reflection:

Pentecost celebrates the **descent of the Holy Spirit** upon the disciples, empowering them to spread the Gospel message with power and understanding. The reading from Acts recounts the miraculous event of speaking in different tongues, symbolizing the universality of the message and the unity of the Church despite cultural and linguistic differences.

Insights:

- The Holy Spirit empowers God's followers to spread the Gospel message and live out their faith with courage and conviction.

- The Church is called to be a beacon of unity and understanding, celebrating diversity while remaining grounded in shared faith in Jesus Christ.

Practical Applications:

- Reflect on the gifts of the Holy Spirit that you possess and how you can use them to serve your community and share the Gospel message.

- Seek opportunities to bridge cultural and linguistic divides, fostering understanding and promoting peace within your community.

- Pray for the continued guidance and presence of the Holy Spirit in your own life and in the Church.

NOTES:_____

_____

_____

_____

_____

_____

_____

_____

_____

_____

_____

_____

_____

_____

_____

_____

_____

_____

Sunday, May 26th:

The Holy Trinity - Solemnity

Bible Readings:

- **First Reading:** Proverbs 8:22-31

- **Psalm:** Psalm 8:5-9

- **Second Reading:** Romans 5:1-5

- **Gospel:** John 16:12-15

Reflection:

This **Solemnity** celebrates the mystery of the **Holy Trinity**: Father, Son, and Holy Spirit, who are three distinct persons existing as one God. The readings offer glimpses into the relationship within the Trinity and its implications   for humanity.

Insights:

- The mystery of the Trinity is beyond full human comprehension, yet it reveals a God who is

- The mystery of the Trinity is beyond full human comprehension, yet it reveals a God who is **relational, loving, and self-giving**. The three persons of the Trinity exist in perfect unity and love, offering a model for human relationships based on love and selflessness.

- The Trinity also signifies **community and inclusivity**. Although distinct persons, the Father, Son, and Holy Spirit are united in their purpose and love, offering a glimpse into God's desire for humanity to live in communion with each other and with him.

Practical Applications:

- While fully understanding the Trinity may be impossible, we can still **approach God with reverence and awe**. Reflect on the implications of a relational and loving God for your own faith and practice.

- Live out the **principles of love and unity** in your daily interactions with others, fostering stronger connections and building a more harmonious community.

- Seek to **deepen your own relationship** with each person of the Trinity through prayer, reflection, and participation in the life of the Church.

NOTES:_____

_____

_____

_____

_____

_____

_____

_____

_____

_____

_____

_____

Sundays in June 2024:

Reflections and Insights

Sunday, June 2nd

(Optional Observance) Corpus Christi - Solemnity

Observed only in the United States

Bible Readings:

- **First Reading:** Exodus 24:3-8

- **Psalm:** Psalm 116:12-19

- **Second Reading:** Hebrews 9:11-15

- **Gospel:** Mark 14:22-26

Reflection:

This **Solemnity** celebrates the **Body and Blood of Christ**, also known as **Corpus Christi**. The readings and the Eucharist itself highlight the significance of Jesus' sacrifice and his real presence in the bread and wine.

Insights:

- The Eucharist is a central sacrament in the Catholic Church, offering a sacred meal to nourish believers and deepen their connection with Christ.

- Through the Eucharist, we encounter Jesus' sacrificial love and receive his grace and strength to live out our faith in daily life.

Practical Applications:

- If you celebrate this Solemnity, participate in the Eucharistic celebration with reverence and devotion.

- Reflect on the significance of the Eucharist in your life and how it nourishes your faith journey.

- Seek opportunities to share the message of Christ's love and sacrifice with others.

NOTES:_____

_____

_____

_____

_____

_____

_____

_____

_____

_____

_____

_____

_____

_____

_____

_____

Sunday, June 9th:

Tenth Sunday in Ordinary Time

Bible Readings:

- **First Reading:** Genesis 3:9-20

- **Psalm:** Psalm 80:2-3, 5-7, 14-17

- **Second Reading:** Romans 5:12-19

- **Gospel:** Mark 4:26-34

Reflection:

This Sunday's readings focus on the themes of **sin, temptation, and God's grace**. The Gospel recounts the parable of the mustard seed, highlighting the power of faith and the potential for growth even from small beginnings.

Insights:

- While we are susceptible to sin and temptation, God's grace is even more powerful, offering forgiveness and the strength to overcome challenges.

- Faith, like the mustard seed, can grow and bear fruit even in seemingly insignificant ways.

Practical Applications:

- Reflect on your own experiences of sin and temptation. Seek forgiveness and rely on God's grace to overcome challenges in your life.

- Nurture your faith through prayer, reflection, and participation in the sacraments, allowing it to grow and bear fruit in your life and in the lives of others.

NOTES:_____

_____

_____

_____

_____

_____

_____

_____

_____

_____

_____

_____

_____

_____

_____

_____

_____

_____

_____

_____

_____

Sunday, June 16th:

Eleventh Sunday in Ordinary Time

Bible Readings:

- **First Reading:** Genesis 14:18-20

- **Psalm:** Psalm 110:1-4, 5-6

- **Second Reading:** 1 Corinthians 11:17-26

- **Gospel:** Mark 5:21-43

Reflection:

This Sunday's readings highlight God's **power and faithfulness** and the importance of **faith** in receiving God's healing and blessings. The Gospel recounts the stories of Jairus' daughter and the woman with a hemorrhage, both experiencing healing through Jesus' touch and their own faith.

Insights:

- God is a source of healing and restoration, offering hope and transformation to those who trust in him.

- Faith is not only believing in God but also trusting his power and goodness, allowing him to work in our lives.

Practical Applications:

- Pray for those in need of healing, both physical and spiritual.

- Offer support and encouragement to those facing challenges or experiencing loss.

- Reflect on your own faith and how you can strengthen it through prayer, scripture reading, and acts of service.

NOTES:_____

_____

_____

_____

_____

_____

_____

_____

_____

_____

_____

_____

_____

_____

_____

_____

_____

_____

_____

Sunday, June 23rd:

Twelfth Sunday in Ordinary Time

Bible Readings:

- **First Reading:** Mark 4:35-41

- **Psalm:** Psalm 107:23-32

- **Second Reading:** Romans 8:26-27

- **Gospel:** Mark 4:35-41

Reflection:

This Sunday's Gospel recounts Jesus calming the storm, highlighting his **power over nature** and his ability to provide peace and calm amidst life's challenges.

Insights:

- Even in the midst of storms and difficulties, God is present and offers us his peace and protection.

- We can turn to God in prayer and trust in his power to guide us through challenging times.

Practical Applications:

- Reflect on the "storms" you face in your own life. Pray for God's peace and guidance to navigate them.

- Offer support and comfort to those facing challenges in their lives.

- Seek opportunities to share the message of hope and peace found in Jesus Christ with others.

NOTES:_____

_____

_____

_____

_____

_____

_____

_____

_____

_____

_____

_____

_____

_____

_____

_____

_____

_____

_____

Sunday, June 30th:

Thirteenth Sunday in Ordinary Time

Bible Readings:

- **First Reading:** 1 Kings 19:14-19

- **Psalm:** Psalm 85:8-14

- **Second Reading:** Romans 8:28-39

- **Gospel:** Mark 5:35-43

Reflection:

This Sunday's readings offer messages of **hope and assurance** in God's unfailing love and presence even in times of doubt or fear. The Gospel recounts Jesus raising Jairus' daughter from the dead, signifying his power over death and his ability to bring new life.

Insights:

- God's love for us is constant and unconditional, regardless of our circumstances or doubts.

- Even in the face of death, God offers hope for new life and resurrection.

Practical Applications:

- Reflect on God's faithfulness in your life, even in times of difficulty.

- Offer hope and encouragement to those who are struggling or feel lost.

- Live a life that reflects God's love and compassion in your interactions with others.

NOTES:_____

_____

_____

_____

_____

_____

_____

_____

_____

_____

_____

_____

_____

_____

_____

_____

_____

_____

_____

_____

Sundays in July 2024:

Reflections and Insights

Bible Readings:

- **First Reading:** Isaiah 66:10-14c

- **Psalm:** Psalm 66:1-3, 5, 8-11

- **Second Reading:** Galatians 6:14-18

- **Gospel:** Luke 10:1-12, 17-20

Reflection:

This Sunday's readings highlight the themes of **joy, service, and mission**. The Gospel recounts Jesus sending out the seventy-two disciples to spread the message of the Kingdom of God.

Insights:

- Following Jesus involves not only receiving his love and grace but also sharing it with others through service and spreading the Gospel message.

- Joy is an essential fruit of Christian life, and it is found in serving God and others with love and compassion.

Practical Applications:

- Reflect on your own gifts and talents.

- Seek opportunities to use your gifts to serve your community and share the love of Christ with others.

- Share your faith journey with others, both through your words and actions, demonstrating the joy and peace found in following Jesus.

NOTES:_____

_____

_____

_____

_____

_____

_____

_____

_____

_____

_____

_____

_____

_____

_____

_____

_____

_____

_____

Sunday, July 14th:

Fifteenth Sunday in Ordinary Time

Bible Readings:

- **First Reading:** Deuteronomy 30:10-14

- **Psalm:** Psalm 119:1-2, 4-5, 7-8, 10-11, 12-13, 14-15

- **Second Reading:** Colossians 1:15-20

- **Gospel:** Luke 10:25-37

Reflection:

This Sunday's Gospel recounts the parable of the Good Samaritan, emphasizing the importance of **love and compassion** for all people, regardless of their background or origin.

Insights:

- Love is the core message of the Christian faith, and it extends beyond our immediate circle or those we consider "neighbors."

- We are called to show love and compassion to everyone we encounter, embodying the example of the Good Samaritan in our daily interactions.

Practical Applications:

- Reflect on your own understanding of "neighbor" and how it might be broader than you initially thought.

- Look for opportunities to show kindness and compassion to those in need, regardless of their background or beliefs.

- Challenge prejudices and biases you may hold towards others, actively seeking to understand and embrace differences.

NOTES:_____

_____

_____

_____

_____

_____

_____

_____

_____

_____

_____

_____

_____

_____

_____

_____

_____

_____

_____

_____

Bible Readings:

- **First Reading:** Genesis 18:1-15a

- **Psalm:** Psalm 15:1-5

- **Second Reading:** Colossians 2:12-14

- **Gospel:** Luke 10:38-42

Reflection:

This Sunday's Gospel recounts the story of **Martha and Mary**, highlighting the importance of **both action and contemplation** in following Jesus.

Insights:

- A balanced Christian life involves both serving others (like Martha) and seeking a deeper relationship with God through prayer and reflection (like Mary).

- We are called to find a balance between our obligations and our spiritual nourishment, allowing both to enrich our lives and faith journey.

Practical Applications:

- Reflect on your own balance between serving others and your personal time for spiritual development.

- Make adjustments in your schedule or priorities to create space for both action and contemplation in your life.

- Encourage others to find a balance that nourishes their own faith journey.

NOTES:_____

_____

_____

_____

_____

_____

_____

_____

_____

_____

_____

_____

_____

_____

_____

_____

_____

_____

_____

_____

_____

_____

Sunday, July 28th:

Seventeenth Sunday in Ordinary Time

Bible Readings:

- **First Reading:** 2 Kings 4:42-44

- **Psalm:** Psalm 145:1-10, 15-18

- **Second Reading:** Ephesians 4:1-6

- **Gospel:** Mark 6:30-34

Reflection:

This Sunday's Gospel recounts Jesus' **compassion** for the crowd who followed him, even after a long day of teaching. He instructs his disciples to provide them with food, demonstrating his concern for their physical and spiritual well-being.

Insights:

- Jesus' compassion extends beyond words and teachings; it translates into action and meeting the needs of those around him.

- We are called to follow Christ's example by showing genuine concern and care for the physical and spiritual well-being of others.

Practical Applications:

- Reflect on the needs of those in your community and around you.

- Seek opportunities to extend a helping hand, whether through acts of service, words of encouragement or simply offering your presence and listening ear.

- Advocate for policies and initiatives that address the needs of the most vulnerable in society, reflecting Christ's compassion in a broader context.

NOTES:_____

_____

_____

_____

_____

_____

_____

_____

_____

_____

_____

_____

_____

_____

_____

_____

_____

_____

_____

_____

Sundays in August 2024:

Reflections and Insights

Sunday, August 4th:

Eighteenth Sunday in Ordinary Time

Bible Readings:

- **First Reading:** Isaiah 55:1-3

- **Psalm:** Psalm 145:8-14, 17-18

- **Second Reading:** Romans 8:31-39

- **Gospel:** Matthew 14:13-21

Reflection:

This Sunday's readings highlight themes of **God's provision, trust, and compassion**. The Gospel recounts the miracle of the feeding of the five thousand, demonstrating Jesus' ability to provide for our needs, even in times of scarcity.

Insights:

- We can trust in God's constant and unfailing provision, even when facing challenges or limitations.

- Jesus meets us in our needs, both physical and spiritual, offering his abundant grace and love.

Practical Applications:

- Reflect on times in your life when you have experienced God's provision, even in unexpected ways.

- Express gratitude for the blessings in your life, no matter how big or small.

- Share your resources and blessings with others in need, demonstrating the compassion you receive from God.

NOTES:_____

_____

_____

_____

_____

_____

_____

_____

_____

_____

_____

_____

_____

_____

_____

_____

_____

_____

_____

Sunday, August 11th:

Nineteenth Sunday in Ordinary Time

Bible Readings:

- **First Reading:** 1 Kings 19:4-8

- **Psalm:** Psalm 34:2-9, 18-19

- **Second Reading:** Ephesians 4:25-5:2

- **Gospel:** Matthew 14:22-33

Reflection:

This Sunday's readings focus on the themes of **faith, perseverance, and reliance on God** in challenging times. The Gospel recounts the story of Peter walking on water, highlighting the importance of faith and trust in Jesus even when faced with fear or doubt.

Insights:

- Following Jesus requires faith and a willingness to step outside our comfort zone.

- Even when faced with challenges or obstacles, we can find strength tand perseverance through reliance on God.

Practical Applications:

- Identify areas of your life where you need to strengthen your faith or trust in God.

- Seek support and encouragement from your faith community in times of difficulty.

- Encourage others facing challenges to find strength and hope in God's presence.

NOTES:_____

_____

_____

_____

_____

_____

_____

_____

_____

_____

_____

_____

_____

_____

_____

_____

_____

_____

Bible Readings:

- **First Reading:** Jeremiah 23:1-6

- **Psalm:** Psalm 23:1-6

- **Second Reading:** Ephesians 2:13-19

- **Gospel:** Matthew 15:21-28

Reflection:

This Sunday's readings emphasize **God's faithfulness and love**, extending to all people regardless of their background or origin. The Gospel recounts the story of the Canaanite woman who persists in her plea for Jesus' healing, challenging stereotypes and prejudices.

Insights:

- God's love and compassion extend beyond boundaries and encompass all people, without discrimination or exclusion.

- Persistence and faith can open doors and lead to unexpected blessings, even when faced with initial resistance.

Practical Applications:

- Examine your own biases and prejudices towards others, and actively seek to challenge them.

- Treat everyone with dignity and respect, recognizing the inherent value and worth in each individual.

- Advocate for inclusivity and justice within your community, ensuring everyone feels welcomed and valued.

NOTES:_____

_____

_____

_____

_____

_____

_____

_____

_____

_____

_____

_____

_____

_____

_____

_____

Sunday, August 25th:

Twenty-First Sunday in Ordinary Time

Bible Readings:

- **First Reading:** Joshua 24:1-3, 14-18

- **Psalm:** Psalm 34:1-10, 22-23

- **Second Reading:** Ephesians 5:15-20

- **Gospel:** Matthew 16:13-23

Reflection:

This Sunday's readings delve into **faith, commitment, and following Jesus**. The Gospel recounts Peter's confession of faith and Jesus' prediction of his suffering and death, challenging the disciples' understanding of the Messiah.

Insights:

- Following Jesus involves not only believing in him but also committing to a life that reflects his teachings, even when it requires sacrifice or goes against popular expectations.

- Facing challenges and difficulties can strengthen our faith and help us deepen our understanding of Jesus' message.

Practical Applications:

- Reflect on your own commitment to following Jesus in your daily life.

- Be prepared to face challenges and obstacles that may come with living out your faith authentically.

- Encourage and support others in their faith journey, offering them companionship and strength in times of difficulty.

NOTES:_____

_____

_____

_____

_____

_____

_____

_____

_____

_____

_____

_____

_____

_____

_____

_____

_____

_____

_____

Sundays in September 2024:

Reflections and Insights

Sunday, September 1st:

Twenty-Second Sunday in Ordinary Time

Bible Readings:

- **First Reading:** Isaiah 35:4-7a

- **Psalm:** Psalm 103:1-8, 10-13

- **Second Reading:** James 2:1-5

- **Gospel:** Mark 7:1-8, 14-15, 21-23

Reflection:

This Sunday's focus is on **true faith and its outward expression in our actions**. The Gospel recounts Jesus' teachings on external vs. internal purity, emphasizing the importance of not only adhering to religious traditions but also living a life consistent with God's love and compassion.

Insights:

- True faith goes beyond following rules or rituals; it manifests in our actions and how we treat others.

- Faithfulness to God translates into living a life of love, justice, and compassion, reflecting his character in our interactions with the world.

Practical Applications:

- Reflect on your own actions and how they align with your faith.

- Seek opportunities to put your faith into action by serving others, promoting justice, and acting with kindness and compassion.

- Challenge yourself to examine your motivations and ensure your actions are driven by genuine love and care for others, not just by religious obligation.

NOTES:_____

_____

_____

_____

_____

_____

_____

_____

_____

_____

_____

_____

_____

_____

_____

_____

_____

_____

Sunday, September 8th:
Twenty-Third Sunday in Ordinary Time

Bible Readings:

- **First Reading:** Nehemiah 8:5-6, 8-10

- **Psalm:** Psalm 19:8-14

- **Second Reading:** 1 Corinthians 12:12-14

- **Gospel:** Luke 16:19-31

Reflection:

This Sunday's readings delve into **themes of wealth, stewardship, and the importance of using our resources wisely.** The Gospel recounts the parable of the rich man and Lazarus, highlighting the dangers of greed and the importance of sharing our blessings with those in need.

Insights:

- Material possessions and wealth are not inherently wrong, but they should not become the ultimate focus or control our lives.

- We are called to be responsible stewards of the resources entrusted to us, using them to help others and further God's kingdom.

Practical Applications:

- Examine your own relationship with material possessions and identify potential areas where you might be placing undue emphasis on them.

- Practice responsible stewardship by sharing your resources with those in need, both financially and through your time and talents.

- Advocate for policies that promote economic justice and address systemic inequalities in wealth distribution.

NOTES:_____

_____

_____

_____

_____

_____

_____

_____

_____

_____

_____

_____

_____

_____

_____

_____

_____

Bible Readings:

- **First Reading:** Ecclesiastes 1:2, 2:21-23

- **Psalm:** Psalm 95:1-5, 7-11

- **Second Reading:** Colossians 3:1-5, 9-11

- **Gospel:** Luke 16:10-13

Reflection:

This Sunday's emphasis is on **faithfulness, responsibility, and living with integrity**. The Gospel recounts Jesus' teaching on trustworthiness and managing earthly possessions with responsibility, reminding us that our faithfulness in small matters reflects our capacity for faithfulness in larger ones.

Insights:

- Being trustworthy in everyday matters is an essential aspect of following Jesus.

- How we manage our earthly possessions reflects our character and prioritizes, revealing where our true loyalty lies.

Practical Applications:

- Reflect on your daily actions and interactions. Are they consistently honest and reflect integrity?

- Practice faithfulness in seemingly insignificant tasks, knowing that your character is built on the foundation of your daily choices.

- Be mindful of how you manage your resources, ensuring they support your values and serve the greater good.

NOTES:_____

_____

_____

_____

_____

_____

_____

_____

_____

_____

_____

_____

_____

_____

_____

_____

_____

_____

Sunday, September 22nd:

Twenty-Fifth Sunday in Ordinary Time

Bible Readings:

- **First Reading:** Wisdom 6:12-16

- **Psalm:** Psalm 119:97-101, 104-105, 112-115

- **Second Reading:** 1 Thessalonians 4:13-18

- **Gospel:** Matthew 24:15-35

Reflection:

This Sunday's themes focus on **hope, vigilance, and preparation for the future**. The Gospel recounts Jesus' discourse on the end times, urging his disciples to remain vigilant and faithful despite challenges.

Insights:

- While the future remains uncertain, we can find hope and strength in our faith and trust in God's presence and care.

- Maintaining a posture of vigilance and preparedness involves living each day faithfully and ethically, regardless of future uncertainties.

Practical Applications:

- Live each day to the fullest, focusing on making positive choices and contributing meaningfully to the present.

- Avoid dwelling on anxieties about the future, choosing instead to trust in God's providence and continue living faithfully.

- Engage in activities and cultivate relationships that bring meaning and purpose to your life, regardless of external circumstances.

NOTES:_____

_____

_____

_____

_____

_____

_____

_____

_____

_____

_____

_____

_____

_____

_____

_____

_____

_____

_____

_____

Bible Readings:

- **First Reading:** Numbers 11:24-29

- **Psalm:** Psalm 18:2-7, 17-20, 28-30, 50

- **Second Reading:** 1 Corinthians 12:4-11

- **Gospel:** Mark 9:38-43, 47-48

Reflection:

This Sunday's readings delve into the importance of **unity, diversity, and using our gifts in service to others**. The Gospel recounts Jesus' teaching on welcoming those who act in his name, even if not part of his immediate circle, and encouraging internal conflict resolution within the community.

Insights:

- The Christian community is diverse, united by faith in Jesus and called to work together despite differences in backgrounds, experiences, and perspectives.

- Each individual within the community possesses unique gifts and talents, meant to be used in service to God and others, building up the collective body of Christ.

Practical Applications:

- Celebrate the diversity within your community and seek opportunities to learn from and appreciate different perspectives.

- Identify your own gifts and talents, and actively seek ways to use them to contribute to the well-being of your community and the world around you.

- Foster conflict resolution within your community through open communication, understanding, and compassion.

NOTES:_____

_____

_____

_____

_____

_____

_____

_____

_____

_____

_____

_____

_____

_____

_____

_____

_____

Sundays in October 2024:

2024:

Reflections and Insights

Sunday, October 6th:

Twenty-Seventh Sunday in Ordinary Time

Bible Readings:

- **First Reading:** Genesis 2:18-24

- **Psalm:** Psalm 84:1-4, 11-12

- **Second Reading:** Hebrews 2:5-11

- **Gospel:** Mark 10:2-16

Reflection:

This Sunday's readings explore the themes of **marriage, commitment, and the sanctity of human relationships**. The Gospel recounts Jesus' teaching on the indissolubility of marriage, emphasizing the importance of commitment and the sacred nature of the marital union.

Insights:

- Marriage is a sacred covenant between individuals, requiring commitment, love, and mutual respect.

- God desires for humanity to experience fulfilling and lasting relationships, reflecting the divine love and unity.

Practical Applications:

- If you are married, reflect on your commitment to your spouse and ways to strengthen your relationship.

- Encourage healthy and respectful relationships within your community, promoting communication, understanding, and forgiveness.

- Advocate for policies and initiatives that support healthy marriages and families, recognizing their vital role in society.

NOTES:_____

_____

_____

_____

_____

_____

_____

_____

_____

_____

_____

_____

_____

_____

_____

_____

Sunday, October 13th:

Twenty-Eighth Sunday in Ordinary Time

Observed only in the United States

Bible Readings:

- **First Reading:** Wisdom 6:12-16

- **Psalm:** Psalm 119:97-101, 104-105, 112-115

- **Second Reading:** 1 Thessalonians 5:1-6

- **Gospel:** Mark 13:24-32

Reflection:

This **Solemnity** in the United States focuses on **Mission Sunday**, emphasizing the importance of **sharing the Gospel message** with the world.

Insights:

- Every Christian is called to participate in the mission of sharing God's love and grace with others, both through words and actions.

- This mission extends beyond geographical boundaries, encompassing the global community and diverse cultures.

Practical Applications:

- Reflect on your own gifts and talents and how you can use them to contribute to the mission of spreading the Gospel.

- Become informed about global needs and challenges, seeking opportunities to support missionary efforts or causes aligned with your values.

- Engage in interfaith dialogue and collaboration, fostering understanding and promoting peace and unity across religious communities.

NOTES:_____

_____

_____

_____

_____

_____

_____

_____

_____

_____

_____

_____

_____

_____

_____

_____

_____

Bible Readings:

- **First Reading:** Exodus 17:8-13

- **Psalm:** Psalm 95:1-5, 7-9

- **Second Reading:** 2 Timothy 3:14-4:5

- **Gospel:** Mark 10:28-31

Reflection:

This Sunday's readings delve into the importance of **faith, perseverance, and trusting in God's providence**. The Gospel recounts Jesus' teaching about following him and the promise of reward for those who do so, even if it involves sacrifice and challenges.

Insights:

- Following Jesus requires faith, a willingness to trust in his guidance even when the path seems uncertain.

- Perseverance in the face of challenges is an essential quality of a Christian life, leading to deeper faith and spiritual growth.

Practical Applications:

- Reflect on your faith journey and identify areas where you may need to strengthen your trust in God's providence.

- Encourage and support others who are facing challenges, reminding them of God's enduring love and faithfulness.

- Remain committed to your values and principles, even when faced with pressures or temptations to compromise them.

NOTES:_____

_____

_____

_____

_____

_____

_____

_____

_____

_____

_____

_____

_____

_____

_____

_____

_____

_____

Sunday, October 27th:

Thirtieth Sunday in Ordinary Time

Bible Readings:

- **First Reading:** Exodus 23:20-23a

- **Psalm:** Psalm 103:1-8, 10-13

- **Second Reading:** Philippians 1:20-24, 27

- **Gospel:** Matthew 22:15-21

Reflection:

This Sunday's theme focuses on **rendering to God what is due to God and rendering to Caesar what is due to Caesar**. The Gospel recounts the challenge posed to Jesus regarding paying taxes, prompting him to emphasize the separation between earthly and heavenly obligations.

Insights:

- While acknowledging earthly authorities and fulfilling our civic duties, we ultimately answer to God and hold him as our highest authority.

- Balancing our responsibilities to both secular and religious spheres requires discernment, prioritizing our ultimate loyalty to God while upholding our roles and obligations in society.

Practical Applications:

- Reflect on your civic duties and actively participate in promoting justice and well-being within your community.

- Be mindful of the potential conflicts arising between societal expectations and your faith, and seek guidance from scripture and prayer when navigating such complexities.

- Engage in dialogue and collaboration with others, fostering understanding and promoting harmonious coexistence within a diverse society.

NOTES:_____

_____

_____

_____

_____

_____

_____

_____

_____

_____

_____

_____

_____

_____

_____

_____

Sundays in November 2024:

Reflections and Insights

Sunday, November 3rd:

Thirty-First Sunday in Ordinary Time

Bible Readings:

- **First Reading:** Proverbs 31:10-31

- **Psalm:** Psalm 128:1-6

- **Second Reading:** Hebrews 11:1-3, 8-12

- **Gospel:** Mark 12:28-34

Reflection:

This Sunday's readings highlight themes of **faith, wisdom, and love**. The Gospel recounts Jesus' teaching on the greatest commandment: to love God with all your heart, soul, and mind, and your neighbor as yourself.

Insights:

- Faith is not only about believing in God, but also about living a life that reflects his love and values.

- Wisdom involves living according to God's principles and making choices that benefit oneself and others.

- Love, the greatest commandment, encompasses both love for God and love for our fellow human beings, regardless of their background or origin.

Practical Applications:

- Reflect on your own understanding and expression of love in your daily life.

- Seek opportunities to show love and compassion to others, through acts of service, kind words, and genuine care.

- Advocate for policies and initiatives that promote social justice and inclusivity, reflecting the love of God that extends to all people.

NOTES:_____

_____

_____

_____

_____

_____

_____

_____

_____

_____

_____

_____

_____

_____

_____

_____

_____

_____

Sunday, November 10th:
Thirty-Second Sunday in Ordinary Time

Bible Readings:

- **First Reading:** Wisdom 6:12-16

- **Psalm:** Psalm 119:97-101, 104-105, 112-115

- **Second Reading:** Hebrews 9:24-28

- **Gospel:** Mark 12:35-37

Reflection:

This Sunday's theme focuses on **recognizing the true presence and nature of God** through faith and understanding. The Gospel recounts Jesus' questioning the religious leaders about the identity of the Messiah, challenging their understanding of the scriptures.

Insights:

- True faith involves not only following rituals or traditions but also seeking a deeper understanding of God's nature and purpose.

- Discernment and critical thinking are crucial in interpreting scriptures and religious teachings, ensuring a deeper and more authentic understanding of God.

Practical Applications:

- Engage in personal and communal study of scripture, seeking a deeper understanding of God's message.

- Engage in open and respectful dialogue with others, even those with different beliefs, fostering understanding and promoting a more inclusive faith journey.

- Be mindful of the potential for misinterpretations and biases in religious traditions, and actively seek authentic sources of knowledge and guidance.

NOTES:_____

_____

_____

_____

_____

_____

_____

_____

_____

_____

_____

_____

_____

_____

_____

_____

_____

_____

_____

_____

Bible Readings:

- **First Reading:** Malachi 3:1-4, 23-24

- **Psalm:** Psalm 24:7-10

- **Second Reading:** 2 Thessalonians 2:1-3, 14-17

- **Gospel:** Mark 9:2-13

Reflection:

This Sunday's readings delve into themes of **faith, perseverance, and the coming of the Kingdom of God**. The Gospel recounts the story of Jesus' transfiguration, highlighting the importance of faith and perseverance in the face of difficulties, leading to the ultimate revelation of God's glory.

Insights:

- Faith helps us navigate challenging times and setbacks, reminding us of God's enduring presence and ultimate purpose.

- Perseverance in following Jesus, even when the path seems unclear, leads to deeper understanding and a closer relationship with him.

Practical Applications:

- Reflect on challenges you are facing currently, drawing strength and hope from your faith and trust in God.

- Encourage and support others who are going through difficulties, reminding them of the transformative power of faith and perseverance.

- Remain committed to your values and principles, even when facing pressure or opposition, trusting in God's guidance and ultimate plan.

NOTES:_____

_____

_____

_____

_____

_____

_____

_____

_____

_____

_____

_____

_____

_____

_____

_____

Sunday, November 24th:

Christ the King - Solemnity

Bible Readings:

- **First Reading:** Ezekiel 34:11-16, 23-24

- **Psalm:** Psalm 23:1-6

- **Second Reading:** Ephesians 1:15-23

- **Gospel:** John 18:33-37

Reflection:

This **Solemnity** celebrates **Christ the King**, emphasizing Jesus' **reign** and **universal kingship**. The Gospel recounts Pilate's questioning of Jesus about his claim to be King, prompting Jesus to clarify the nature of his kingdom and its focus on truth and service.

Insights:

- Jesus' kingship does not rely on earthly power or dominance, but on love, truth, and service.

- The reign of Christ transcends earthly boundaries and encompasses all people, offering hope, love, and salvation to the world.

Practical Applications:

- Reflect on your own understanding of leadership and how it aligns with the principles of Christ's kingship, emphasizing service, compassion, and love.

- Advocate for justice, peace, and equality, striving to embody the values of Christ's kingdom in your daily interactions with others.

- Share the message of Christ's love and hope with the world, promoting understanding and fostering a more just and compassionate society.

NOTES:_____

_____

_____

_____

_____

_____

_____

_____

_____

_____

_____

_____

_____

_____

_____

_____

_____

_____

Sundays in December 2024:

Reflections and Insights

Sunday, December 1st:

First Sunday of Advent

Bible Readings:

- **First Reading:** Isaiah 2:1-5

- **Psalm:** Psalm 122:1-9

- **Second Reading:** Romans 13:11-14

- **Gospel:** Mark 13:24-37

Reflection:

This Sunday marks the beginning of the **Advent season**, a time of **preparation and anticipation** for the birth of Jesus Christ. The Gospel reading highlights the importance of **vigilance and readiness** for the coming of the Lord.

Insights:

- Advent is a call to prepare our hearts and minds for the coming of Christ, both in the celebration of his birth and in his eventual return.

- We are called to be vigilant, staying awake and alert to the presence of God in our lives.

Practical Applications:

- Engage in activities that deepen your faith and spiritual growth during the Advent season, such as prayer, scripture reading, and reflection.

- Make time for introspection and reflect on areas where you can prepare yourself for Christ's coming, both personally and as a community.

- Extend acts of kindness and compassion to others, reflecting the spirit of the season and preparing the world for the message of hope and love brought by Christ.

NOTES:_____

_____

_____

_____

_____

_____

_____

_____

_____

_____

_____

_____

_____

_____

_____

_____

_____

_____

_____

Sunday, December 8th:

Second Sunday of Advent

Bible Readings:

- **First Reading:** Isaiah 11:1-10

- **Psalm:** Psalm 72:1-7, 10-14

- **Second Reading:** Romans 15:4-13

- **Gospel:** Matthew 3:1-12

Reflection:

This Sunday focuses on the theme of **hope** associated with the coming of the Messiah. The Gospel recounts John the Baptist's preaching, urging repentance and preparation for the arrival of Jesus.

Insights:

- Advent invites us to rediscover hope, both in the promise of the new life brought by Christ and in the potential for transformation in our own lives.

- John the Baptist's call for repentance encourages us to acknowledge our shortcomings and open ourselves to the transformative power of Christ's message.

Practical Applications:

- Reflect on your own hopes and aspirations for the future, allowing them to be enriched by the hope offered by the coming of Christ.

- Practice gratitude for the blessings in your life, even amidst challenges, and share that joy with others.

- Engage in acts of reconciliation and forgiveness, seeking to create a more peaceful and hopeful world in preparation for Christ's arrival.

NOTES:_____

_____

_____

_____

_____

_____

_____

_____

_____

_____

_____

_____

_____

_____

_____

_____

_____

_____

_____

_____

Sunday, December 15th:

Third Sunday of Advent

Bible Readings:

- **First Reading:** Isaiah 35:1-6a, 10

- **Psalm:** Psalm 146:6-9, 10-11

- **Second Reading:** James 5:7-10

- **Gospel:** Matthew 11:2-11

Reflection:

This Sunday, known as **Gaudete Sunday**, is a moment of **joy and anticipation** amidst the Advent season. The Gospel recounts John the Baptist sending messengers to Jesus, seeking confirmation of his identity as the Messiah.

Insights:

- This Sunday reminds us that even during times of preparation and waiting, there is room for joy and celebration.

- Recognizing Jesus as the Messiah brings hope and assurance, prompting anticipation for his arrival and the blessings he brings.

Practical Applications:

- Find moments of joy and celebration in your life during the Advent season, allowing them to be a source of strength and hope.

- Share your joy with others through acts of kindness, generosity, and spreading the message of hope embodied by Christ.

- Reflect on the reasons for your faith and allow them to be a source of personal joy and encouragement throughout the year.

NOTES:_____

_____

_____

_____

_____

_____

_____

_____

_____

_____

_____

_____

_____

_____

_____

_____

_____

_____

Sunday, December 22nd:

Fourth Sunday of Advent

Bible Readings:

- **First Reading:** Micah 5:1-4a

- **Psalm:** Psalm 80:1-7, 17-19

- **Second Reading:** Hebrews 10:5-10

- **Gospel:** Luke 1:26-38

Reflection:

This Sunday, known as **Stir-Up Sunday**, encourages preparation for the **Nativity of Jesus**. The Gospel recounts the Annunciation, the announcement by the angel Gabriel to Mary that she would bear the Son of God.

Insights:

- The Annunciation signifies the beginning of God's plan for salvation, and as we approach Christmas, we are called to stir ourselves and prepare our hearts to receive it.

- Mary's willingness to accept her role in God's plan serves as an inspiration for faith

- Mary's willingness to accept her role in God's plan serves as an inspiration for faith and obedience, reminding us to say "yes" to God's call in our own lives.

Practical Applications:

- Engage in activities that foster a sense of anticipation and preparation for the celebration of Christmas.

- Reflect on your own role in God's plan and how you can contribute to spreading his message of love and hope in the world.

- Practice acts of service and generosity, reflecting the spirit of the season and embodying the humility and compassion of Mary.

NOTES:_____

_____

_____

_____

_____

_____

_____

_____

_____

_____

_____

_____

_____

_____

_____

_____

_____

Sunday, December 29th:

The Holy Family - Feast

Bible Readings:

- **First Reading:** Sirach 3:2-6, 12-14

- **Psalm:** Psalm 128:1-6

- **Second Reading:** Colossians 3:12-21

- **Gospel:** Luke 2:41-52

Reflection:

This **Feast** celebrates the **Holy Family** of Jesus, Mary, and Joseph, highlighting the importance of family life and its role in faith formation. The Gospel recounts the story of Jesus finding himself in the temple at the age of twelve, demonstrating his unique connection to God while still respecting his earthly family.

Insights:

- The Holy Family serves as a model for love, respect, and faith within the family unit.

- The concept of family extends beyond biological ties to encompass the broader community of faith and those who share our values.

Practical Applications:

- Nurture your relationships with family members, fostering love, respect, and communication.

- Extend acts of support and care to those who may be alone or without family, creating a sense of belonging and community.

- Reflect on your own role in the family of faith, contributing to its growth and fostering a sense of unity and compassion among its members.

NOTES:_____

_____

_____

_____

_____

_____

_____

_____

_____

_____

_____

_____

_____

_____

_____

_____

_____

_____

Appendix

In this appendix, we provide additional resources and tools to further enhance your understanding and engagement with the Catholic Sunday Mass Readings for 2024. These resources include a glossary of terms to help clarify any unfamiliar terminology, a liturgical calendar for the year 2024 to provide context for the readings.

Additional Resources

1. **Catechism of the Catholic Church**: A comprehensive summary of the Catholic faith, including teachings on Scripture, sacraments, morality, and prayer.

2. **Compendium of the Catechism of the Catholic Church**: A concise question-and-answer format that presents the essentials of Catholic doctrine.

3. **The Bible**: The Word of God, containing the Old and New Testaments, which serve as the foundation for Catholic teaching and worship.

4. **Daily Reflections**: Various books, websites, and apps offer daily reflections on the Scripture readings of the day, providing insights and spiritual guidance for daily prayer and meditation.

5. **Online Resources**: Websites such as the United States Conference of Catholic Bishops (USCCB) offer a wealth of resources related to the liturgy, including daily readings, prayers, and reflections.

6. **Spiritual Classics**: Timeless works by saints and spiritual writers, such as St. Augustine, St. Teresa of Avila, and St. Thomas Aquinas, provide deep insights into the Christian life and the mysteries of faith.

Glossary of Terms

- **Advent**: The liturgical season of preparation for the coming of Christ, both at Christmas and in anticipation of His second coming.

- **Liturgical Year**: The annual cycle of seasons and feasts in the Catholic Church, which includes Advent, Christmas, Lent, Easter, and Ordinary Time.

- **Gospel**: The teachings and life of Jesus Christ as recorded in the four Gospels of the New Testament: Matthew, Mark, Luke, and John.

- **Psalm**: A sacred song or hymn found in the Book of Psalms in the Old Testament, traditionally attributed to King David.

- **Eucharist**: The sacrament of the body and blood of Christ, also known as the Mass or Holy Communion.

- **Liturgy**: The official public worship of the Church, which includes the celebration of the Mass, the Liturgy of the Hours, and other sacramental rites.

- **Lectionary**: A book containing the Scripture readings appointed for each day of the liturgical year, used in the celebration of the Mass and other liturgical rites.

Liturgical Calendar for 2024

The liturgical calendar for the year 2024 provides an overview of the major feasts and seasons of the Church year. This calendar serves as a guide for understanding the context of the Sunday Mass Readings and for planning liturgical celebrations and devotions throughout the year.

Here is the Liturgical Calendar for 2024:

January

- **1st:** New Year's Day (Solemnity of Mary, Mother of God) - **Image of The Solemnity of Mary, Mother of God**

- **6th:** Epiphany of the Lord

- **14th:** The Baptism of the Lord

February

- **10th:** Ash Wednesday

- **17th:** First Sunday of Lent

- **24th:** Second Sunday of Lent

March

- **3rd:** Third Sunday of Lent

- **10th:** Fourth Sunday of Lent (Laetare Sunday)

- **17th:** Fifth Sunday of Lent (Passion Sunday)

- **24th:** Palm Sunday of the Passion of the Lord

- **29th:** Holy Thursday

- **30th:** Good Friday

- **31st:** Holy Saturday

April

- **1st:** Easter Sunday

- **8th:** Second Sunday of Easter (Divine Mercy Sunday)

- **15th:** Third Sunday of Easter

- **22nd:** Fourth Sunday of Easter (Good Shepherd Sunday)

- **29th:** Fifth Sunday of Easter (Rogation Sunday)

May

- **5th:** Sixth Sunday of Easter

- **12th: Ascension Sunday - Image of Ascension Sunday**

- **19th:** Seventh Sunday of Easter (Pentecost Sunday)

- **26th:** Most Holy Trinity Sunday

June

- **2nd:** The Body and Blood of Christ (Corpus Christi)

- **9th:** Second Sunday of Ordinary Time

- **16th:** Third Sunday of Ordinary Time

- **23rd:** Fourth Sunday of Ordinary Time

- **30th:** Fifth Sunday of Ordinary Time

July

- **7th:** Sixth Sunday of Ordinary Time

- **14th:** Seventh Sunday of Ordinary Time

- **21st:** Eighth Sunday of Ordinary Time

- **28th:** Ninth Sunday of Ordinary Time

August

- **4th:** Tenth Sunday of Ordinary Time

- **11th:** Eleventh Sunday of Ordinary Time

- **18th:** Twelfth Sunday of Ordinary Time

- **25th:** Thirteenth Sunday of Ordinary Time

September

- **1st:** Fourteenth Sunday of Ordinary Time

- **8th:** Fifteenth Sunday of Ordinary Time

- **15th:** Sixteenth Sunday of Ordinary Time

- **22nd:** Seventeenth Sunday of Ordinary Time

- **29th:** Eighteenth Sunday of Ordinary Time

October

- **6th:** Nineteenth Sunday of Ordinary Time

- **13th:** Twentieth Sunday of Ordinary Time

- **20th:** Twenty-First Sunday of Ordinary Time

- **27th:** Twenty-Second Sunday of Ordinary Time

November

- **3rd:** Twenty-Third Sunday of Ordinary Time

- **10th:** Twenty-Fourth Sunday of Ordinary Time

- **17th:** Twenty-Fifth Sunday of Ordinary Time

- **24th: Christ the King Sunday** (if it falls on the same day as the Twenty-Sixth Sunday of Ordinary Time, Christ the King Sunday takes precedence) - **Image of Christ the King Sunday**

December

- **1st:** First Sunday of Advent

- **8th:** Second Sunday of Advent

- **15th:** Third Sunday of Advent (Gaudete Sunday)

- **22nd:** Fourth Sunday of Advent

- **25th:** Christmas Day (Solemnity of the Nativity of the Lord)

Made in the USA
Monee, IL
25 August 2024

64570641R00083